AUTOWAR

AUTOWAR

Assiyah Jamilla Touré

Brick Books

Library and Archives Canada Cataloguing in Publication

Title: Autowar / Assiyah Jamilla Touré.
Names: Touré, Assiyah Jamilla, author.
Description: Poems.
Identifiers: Canadiana (print) 20210225661 | Canadiana (ebook) 20210225769 | ISBN 9781771315630 (softcover) | ISBN 9781771315647 (HTML) | ISBN 9781771315654 (PDF)
Classification: LCC PS8639.O9685 A98 2021 | DDC C811/.6—dc23

We gratefully acknowledge the Canada Council for the Arts, the Government of Canada through the Canada Book Fund, and the Ontario Arts Council for their support of our publishing program.

Canada Council for the Arts | Conseil des arts du Canada

ONTARIO ARTS COUNCIL
CONSEIL DES ARTS DE L'ONTARIO
an Ontario government agency
un organisme du gouvernement de l'Ontario

Government of Canada | Gouvernement du Canada

The book is set in Sabon Pro and ITC Avant Garde Gothic.
Designed by Emma Allain.
Printed and bound by Coach House Printing.

BRICK BOOKS
487 King St. W.
Kingston, ON
K7L 2X7
www.brickbooks.ca

Though much of the work of Brick Books takes place on the ancestral lands of the Anishinaabeg, Haudenosaunee, Huron-Wendat, and Mississaugas of the Credit peoples, our editors, authors, and readers from many backgrounds are situated from coast to coast to coast in Canada on the traditional and unceded territories of over six hundred nations who have cared for Turtle Island from time immemorial. While living and working on these lands, we are committed to hearing and returning the rightful imaginative space to the poetries, songs, and stories that have been untold, under-told, wrongly told, and suppressed through colonization.

For the triplets.

I hope this book is confusing, foreign,
and strange to you.

CONTENTS

beckoning

abandon me
i might retain the knife-wield of my aches
above you or any god is the taste of my own wound

this wrongness has been in me from time
i bow to it and it caresses me with lashes

it is overwhelming for me to be almost loved
every conflict is terrorism for me
i am in fear of the coming and goings
i taste the rot on every fruit

i run on silences
i swallow them whole, eagerly
see? i seem to say

a steady heartbeat taming my ear
is an assault
my recall is quartered
by any steadfastness

the insistence of another blood-filled body

beckoning, trapping

holding, releasing

beckoning

trapping me

wishing is not the same as wanting

fighting is taking the peel of peace
fighting skins peace in the cold

fighting slakes a thirst for peace
an honourable fight to death for silence

peace is adjacent to theory
me looking for peace is learning theory
learning a theory of hunger
never having been not hungry

is this it?
i ask the musk
my nose is searching
buried in the nape
of another animal

is this it?
i ask, watering that dead plant
flooding my apathy with the
fertilizer dregs of my will

scraped out the corpse i'm feeding

i look for peace everywhere i go
                    i look for it in all the wrong places
is this it?
grinding my body
pathetically, against
your body

is this it? muffled
i ask myself face down
in my bed trying to disappear
crushing my body down

i know i don't have to fight but old habits die hard

is this all? in my head
not even really breathing
just wanting to choke myself
so bad, is this all?

is this all there is?

acidfield

bones jutting up jagged planted in this garden
will we too be a garden on the ocean floor
an ocean so acidic, vast, roaring
the salt shearing everything in it to bone
bones for us to be too, tomorrow?
or something new where bones used to be?

caught breath, lost boasts, portraits
forgotten words now imprinted on relics
locked up somewhere in abandoned houses
in abandoned cities, empty strongholds, fortresses

a sharp planet, all sulphur, burns everything in it
all of it a pending pre-excavation
our little lived lives in forever copies
for them to dust off and upload later
argue over who we were
bloodthirst stirring

note we are fluent in lies
accuse with citrine jewels

congregating crushed small fish together
speaking only to ourselves and starving at length
saying, *i will feed on the grey gaze of your hunger*
stretching to dry ourselves in the sun, slathered in thin atmosphere
we'll die anyway, the in-between doesn't matter
our face will be still, our eyes unrippling

frosted glass stereograms, radiating wondrous rows
when we arrange our powdery chalk skeletons
if a husk is an outer shell, our bones
will be husks for air and children passing
will look upon the sweet cane
sugar yellow of our once bodies

they'll run through fields of us
passing finger over femur
like we once did to our own yellow fields of grasses

disturbing our hollow bones
they will dig us up
dig up our worlds of weariness
we will prove once again that time is still
alive as ever, just a little more quiet now
so that when the softness of their fingers

disturbs our weary ends and endings
we are unsettled, touched, disquieted

that's why you and i tremble now
seeking warmth any old where
that we can find it

nocturnal

of course, that song "kalise"
passing rhythms up and down its chords
imagines her white haired and orange skinned
with feather-light bird bones slicking

errant sailors mistaking the manatee
for a goddess or princess or warm body
we, audiences, see creatures swimming in others
and avert our eyes and lend them our shyness

we are aghast at the nakedness of animals
we demand it until we are sick with it—we are feral

we could be animals again if we wanted
maybe we do, and that's where we're headed
a suicide mission? kamikaze society?
give us disaster—let's shoot each other with sticks again

i hear kalise and see voluminous soft bodies brown
coloured and gleaming

passing rhythms up and down their chords
ribs aching the arrangement

    i look down and see kalise
        swimming in my body

    i sway side to side in front of the vanity
i oscillate between self-idolatry and loathing
        there is hibiscus in my hair, an affectation
  i do not smell of anything except
soap and my skin—

    it is red earth, an alert
    it—clay-soft armour—is an exclamation
    my dark limb beckons at predation
                my skin slipping folds me into night
            light sliding over and off of me

outside my window is a garden in a world of gardens
leaves bigger than all of me and my meagre riches
these leaves in some other place enshrined me

a temple of leaves, a sceptre of stalk, lace
            behind them mauve and maybe water hanging

i cut that air with the song of me breathing

i grasp at air like i'm up from a deep dive

nocturnal

i water my lungs, panting in lead

in the heavy dark

idolatry

cut the interest off the top of what my body earns
these uninsured appendages still gleaming
    my copywritten twitter bio has pull
        i'm bingeing on their faux worship currency

these earnings are meagre but mine
this squalor is earned and this hunger becomes me
i'm painting a still life of myself stagnating

printing a life on high gloss with filters and passes
forever fumbling for the next reinvention
the branding of this body is chaos magic

i am an approachable object—a carved wooden idol
if i am a deity i am of the rank closest to dirt

a blue fire has pressed to my clay limbs
listen for the hardening and ageing of me

somebody overspiced and overpriced the pot
once sharp, now it is battered to bitterness

a little more acerbic if i allowed it
i have been sick for a while now

i gulp air to dilute the poison
nevermind that it is the poison
nevermind that i drink the poison
i am transplendent, glittering

it glows from my chest—i am three hearted
i am clamorous, chaotic—altared on phones
these meagre earnings are mine
maybe i haven't been sick for a while now
i'm a vessel and my holdings disarm me
drink from me

let's both pretend we're somewhere else—
here's you and me in a race car
here's you and me on tandem theory
here's looking at you, child

we'll pretend to be nonchalant—
what about sungazing, or what i call looking at you, kid
what about the sensation of being "good"
the overdosing on being "good"

and i'll pretend to want the truth—
i'm always afraid that i'm being watched
yo of course i'm being watched
those disembodied eyes are unbearable

i will start an autocult of naivety
everyone gets one last chalice
i will perform this until it feels real
repeat the movements—sidewalks, bus stops, stages

my brain is split and i am stretching
my spirit is repelled when we are touching
let's have all our conversations under this
white sheet with the light coming through

i am not tight my body dislikes you
don't come round here no more
i'm checked all way the hell out
moored on this mattress

if they ask why i did it
tell them it was for the sun
beyond the sun i have need of nothing
i'll eat nothing else, sungazing

will i become her?
her me?

i will stand in her rays
no more milk, honey, dates
i won't consume anything at all
whose thinnest layer is not translucent

i can only drink water
only drink air
only gasp for breath
only pant for air
pant for air on the shore

on the shore, gills trembling
on the shore where i'm slowing
bowing

deflating on the sharp rocks there
giving all my effects over
to stillness

practice

i can handmake myself into a gift
call me a performance artist

the physical experience of my body in it every sense disturbed

i can hear tastes now
simulated life has new meaning

how does one practice rhetoric, when i am a ritual rhetorical practice

my hands are pixelated, my trembling is degradation

even my arrival is praxis, i practice arrival and call it cumming

i am rooted, i practice stillness
i uproot myself, i compost myself

i cut my hair i save my hair i break my hair
i fondle it
it's soft if i touch it soft

i live here in front of the looking glass

live for the glare of my little talking box

i practice knowing for the camera

i practice a charming look for them

a charming look that gives them the sense that i am knowing

a charming smile a playful eye

i am a nymph mother, baby god

i am so good at this game i can play it asleep, on autopilot

i can be a false idol on autopilot

i am so good it is above me

this game is almost over anyway, it's a persistent coded countdown

i've gotten all the use out of me

i am worn out and have warred enough

i am not greedy enough for this

i don't want to be full anymore

i have gorged on what for nothing

i have hoarded nothing for it

i have grown a velvet coarseness

i am crushed

even my callouses are crushed

my hands are

peeling and

peeling and

disintegrating

bloodthirst

here in the dark
i am insatiable for my flesh
i just can't get enough of me
all my tiny after-wounds
hard crust of goodness come up
my shell throws up scabs of pavement
they are so sweet in opening to me
that's me giving, still too soft
for the poor brittleness of my teeth

an empty space

i.

inventing white knights, fathers in strangers
positive celebrity paternity tests, soap operas
eternities of happy endings, of long losts, of destinies

when i was a kid i'd say, my father is a race car
my father is if ike turner and blade had a baby

i'd say, when my father sneezes he covers his mouth like this
i'd say, he doesn't like hugs
his favourite movie is jaws, he was in the army

a father is a neat cinematic solution
the solution is simply an aesthetic of a solution
the nuclear family is a modern paraphilia
a white picketed invention
the fetish of the death of the village

ii.

a missing shape
an empty space

of white athletic crew socks
of brown khakis and corduroy
of noxious cologne

each hair of a moustache is humorous
        though the whole apparatus is void of humour
laughter is made
        in quelling laughter
a coffee, whiskey
        bitter beer
the pun aesthetic
        the most fun aesthetic
the father prosthetic

                        the michael jackson poster
                        the cover of the soundtrack to free willy

love me and feed me
kiss me and free me

iii.

one where
i sit in your lap and
you rock me to sleep

one that's the same
except i'm crying
til i'm not anymore

where
you sing me your favourite rock song
from when hendrix came to africa on vinyl

my mother tells you about her day
after we'll do mine

she kisses
one eye
you kiss the other
you carry me

one where you carry me because
i fell asleep

when we were guests

at a friend's house

you carry me just because

i am getting so big!

i am getting so big but

you carry me anyway

just because

iv.

theory of
        vertical hierarchy

time being non-linear and all
the higher up a man is the more powerful

ever since my dad died i haven't had one bad luck day not even once
        being supposed to die but didn't is a good luck day

theory of my daddy can love me better dead

        he can take better care of me
        from heaven

other i

all virtual realities being made of tiny shapes stacked together
is this all a polygonal world of edges, angles, hard cubic trappings
what with time being a solid edge
and not a blurry painting like we thought
and this reality virtual, unassuming

don't think too hard about this not being real
who plugs into a game for a pretend life of suffering?
no one would upload into a rigged bout, no lives
inventory empty, enemies mechanical, lying in wait

is this edge closer than it may appear?
i too am split, fallen over, no clip
an accidentally symmetrical bisection
my parts all on display—a plaything

other i   i too am at this edge
                    in this moment
                              elsewhere
writing this, a poem
                    and that poem, there

and somewhere else writing one better

one that would do better there than here

would i do better there than here?

will i be a little richer

softer or harder

more ready to fight

less small, less borrowed

every bit as dark, but a little less black?

not quite as crushed into a bow

more deliciously numb, less of that aura leak

a smooth inner peace like a pond evading

deep disappointment with ethereal clarity

an objective distance from the order of things

given over to whatever seems natural

which we call whatever feels good

whatever feels like winning

i pace every street, looking for

anything that looks like my front door

a little less imagining home pieced up from

archived youtube music videos
spun into background noise for parties

national geographic ephemera for future offenders
to press me between the pages of

a little less honour needed to go home
a few less killings needed for honour
a little less purity needed
worthiness is weakness

there—sipping my burned tongue
in another chance at a village somewhere
another possibility of being somewhere
a soft city edge and our gleaming vessels trailing

here am i, who can sit
with their back to the door
without tensing to sprint
like a car in a cage

somewhere unreachable but that i know like
every place i ever dreamed of
places i've only eaten at in friends' anecdotes

anywhere i'm copy-pasted in the background of a story

a mess of free associations—elastic memory

the bite of metal dogging me

sparks whenever i eat

metal on metal

here am i braving crowds

unterrified of

    other people

here are other people

    worthy of weakness

unknown and unknowing of me

here are others, characters same as me

inventory empty, no lives

playthings

flinch

content warning: sexual violence

white men love me
white men love me
white men love me

so much white men love me
so much white men love me
so much white men love me until

love me til they can't white men
love me til they don't white men
love me til they hate me blame me

white men hate me so much
white men hate me when they
hate me it is so much

it is so much it is so much
white men hate to see me
white men hate to see me go

even when they love to watch me

walk away they hate to see me
white men love to see me hurt

white men love to see me white men
love to see me flinch away
love to hurt me til i flinch away

white men hate me for me
hate to have me go white men
hate to see me go

white men need me close
white men like to hurt me
white men love to hurt me

white men love to hurt me close
love to have me close
love to see me flinch up close

white men love to touch me
touch me til i flinch up close
make me flinch so they can feel me flinch up close

white men love to touch me white men

who purport to love me love to touch me white men
who purport to love me love to shove their fingers in me

while i am asleep white men
love to touch me awake til i push them away

white men love to shove their fingers in me
love to shove heave grip crush

white men love to claim they shoved
their fingers in me while i was asleep
because they have sexsomnia

white men with sexsomnia
love to fall asleep near women who don't
know they have sexsomnia

white men love to call a lie
white men love to not believe me
white men love to believe

other white men over me, a lie
lie in wait a row of white men
think i am a lie like to see me

give up on the lie, give up on me

white men love to see me give up
white men love to see me back down
white men love to see me

step back down, run back down
white men loom on landings
take steps down, shove it down

turn my eyes away white
men love to see me back
away white men love to see me leave

white men love to see me
white men love to see me
over facetime white men love to beg

for me to touch myself over facetime
white men love to touch themselves to me touching myself
over facetime white men love to do this

white men love to do this at work
under their desk at work white men love

to see me white men love to do this

white men love to do this in the car
white men love to do it in the car
white men love to do this in bed

next to their wife white men love to do this
next to their now wife who they met after me
next to their now wife who is post-me

after they met me and begged me to touch myself
to themselves touching themselves to me
touching myself over facetime

white men love to see me be another me
for them white men love to see me be their me
for them white men love me touching myself for them

white men love to see me be their fantasy
white men love their little fantasies white men
love a million little fantasies by way of me

white men love a clear path white men
love this body love to walk this body white men

love a clear path of a body or post-body

for white men who like to touch themselves
to me touching myself over facetime
cut to me touching myself over facetime

for me touching myself over facetime
touching myself for white men to see
for white men to see me to see me

is white men loving me
is white men loving me
is white men loving me
is white men loving me
is white men loving me
is white men loving me
is white men loving me

physics

my first pillow is the landmark
the turn in the path is also the crook
of my mother's arm and the back of that same hand

i remember when i was so small my mother's legs
were indistinguishable from mountains
i was unaffected by the deaths of animals
i liked the giving over of gaiety
i'd leave my body and
float off the balcony

the skin of my face and my mother's palm
are both striking, they are the same, atomically
the physics are phenomenal the energy transfer and collision

i am reeling! gravitational pull   years seeking that same perfect
combination of tenderness and pain
in every passing intimacy

i too remember a second where you reached for me
and grasped me almost painfully tight, you and i

crossing the freeway with my wrist in a vice

and my hand is still there
it's still there in yours years later

everything has happened but
we are still crossing that freeway

i'll leave my body to visit your hands
indistinguishable from deserts

touch is an
anchor

polychaete

we have erected new villages now
we love our unsightly children
just a little less, and a little less brightly
should the beauty of self-possession evade them

            we like the suggestion of a pedigreed corpse
            more than the pretext of lived unsightly joy

having bred dogs into helpless creatures
we flatter and powder ourselves
with their dependence on us
this is called hedging your bets

            we like their injuries prefracture
            longing to be their farmers and raise them
            demanding the ribbon for swollen bets

we are inclined to love our ugly mannered child less
and put all the little we beg at the foot of beauty

a worm writhing in the rain
is an abomination to every bitter sense

a worm writhing in a bin
buys anthropomorphy through use

a worm writhing in one's sex
buys utility through use

a worm writhing on the ocean floor
a polychaete, transcends its station
by moving to different places
and undulating within instead of out
and has a beautiful thrill of organic lace
trussed up around one end of its body
which is pure white wedding silk like
all those tiny ancient fossils
that make the fine sand on the ocean floor

a true ecoterrorist
would change all the animals
and insects and birds and invertebrates
into uselessly beautiful

or beautifully useless
to help us hedge our bets

i don't like the earth
until i'm nutrient starved to craving dirt
until it feeds and fucks me to sleep

once i am lulled by its electric murmurings
it adorns me in a necklace of rope

snakeskin

they shed their skin
shed their skin skin
                    shed their body's body, shed their corpses

let them on let them go on
wear wear worn on
                    let them go on

dry husk hanging petals
blush night-ning near
flat moist crescent beat
beat open flesh holy
                    a meat temple hook hanging

a physical site is not sacrifice
blood lingering, body sight
plot of earth weighing my belly
                    burial ground for my mouth only

bleached white battle moors
we die far from home now

wasted, wan, winding tracks left
                    spiralling patterns, flushing, earth, feet left

on until the next thrill, rush of living
monochrome metal armour racing sides bleeding
they are all eternally cutting chafing
                    always for the roughness of each other

those that shed are easy now, cup out
for us to pour one so let them go on
peeling their injuries, peeling, go on
                    let them heal wrong

bury the lede and never say
they took the blows they fought for
                              (give rest their tattered skins)
so beautifully battled   lay them down and
leave their earthly shells where they shed them

i don't shed tears for them
don't waste water for skin, pouring out for dry clay
see they shed their skin, shed their skin skin
shed their body's body, shed their corpses

fruit are peeled down to the goodness

to the newest, to the goodest

colossal

attuned
i know touch is impossible

colossal space edging matter
too big for longing now

it's not recoiling from touch
it's seeking the sensation of nothing

i am not afraid—i just don't feel anything
everything is wrung out of
violent relief anyway

i want to hold on to this quietness

and keep on and on
and on and on

rehearsal

content warning: sexual violence

act 1:

some things don't get said
this demolition is one of them
one of the ones
you don't get to say

put a whole lot in
front and behind it
water it down in post
it'll go down easy for the rest now

pile on reasons, explanations
a series of subtractions, distractions
market the event
pigs in a blanket

when we talk about the revenant
we only talk about the bear
just say allen, don't talk soon-yi
we only do sunsets, never a sunrise

act 2:

i was raped.
don't use it to entertain yourself
pity is a drug
i was raped before then and i was raped after then.

most of my life has taken place between rapes
i have been raped so many times
that before i was sick of being raped
i craved it

act 3:

i was not held after my rape
i have not yet been held after my rape
i have not been comforted post-rape
nobody has held me

i have not been allowed to unravel
there has not been time
i have asserted monetary value
i have been a very busy girl

denouement:

(in decades i'll learn that i am no victim of violence, i am adrift on violence, i am immersed in violence, i take on violence, i seek it, i am violence, my fear is violent, i seek harm, i embody harm to myself and others, i seek harm. it multiplies, infects. is hungry. i shed the romance of victimhood. i survey the damages. i am all of the aftermath. i am the damages. i did the damages. i am the damages. i do the damages. i am the damages)

being raped after a rape
after a rape that will not be undone
is a little like being held after a rape
a rape that is just a rehearsal, now.

the intimacy of absence

in a shared accident you can be impaled
by the broken body of those with whom
you are breaking your final breath

those of us who are unafraid
of the stoic promise of collision
will make like the birds do instead

live our lives in patterns and
murmurations, swallow one another up
in the caress of a million other bodies
racing to close the gap then collapsing away

in the final stretch, you and i, roped by tides, never colliding

you and i have the best secret of all
we are not any better when we love
we can do it all from far away

we can love each other in avoidance
we like the memory of pulling away

pulling away will be a pull on me
because i'll remember you fondly for that
i'll give you nothing that you can hold

let's stay friends in url
and never let on what we know
years after all we've almost seen
when we cross one and other

melting into the wallpaper
of too-hot ballrooms and dives
as prize for having dodged yours
blessings condensate on mine

two to tear me away from the thrill of your silence
solar plexus filled to bursting
pregnant pauses, heavy with promise
sliding in any corner that'll welcome me
nestled between two hard walls
it is firm, and will do to mimic your presence
we might miss ourselves again

off-track after all these races
where do we run to without one another

lost without my mechanical hare
i might search your face in crowds
and wonder at your absence
idle thoughts passing over you unseeing
i might miss you here, one day again
but not if i see you first
but not if i see you first

fetishes

my body overflows
fills my room with soiled clothing, dead plants
books to have and never crack but look at

the fine salvaged china piles in the stainless tub
my little lucite cube table is an empty pride

and the empties stand to attention
posing coyfully like little dolls, soldiers—all habit repetitions

aloe vera juice
aloe vera juice
aloe vera juice

if i die here and am worthy
they will freeze everything in time
insert little plaques with conceptual statements

here is where they knocked their
mango nectar juice box
and spilled incense dust on their

cream low-profile sectional
and dropped a single-serve blue jam
then stepped in it
over and over
until it made its own dark scar
on the landscape

arizona green
tea arizona green
tea arizona green

will they see me reflected in all this garbage?

it's the manner in which
my inner rot seeps out
to even my nice things
they all start beauteous
they enter this kingdom

once deeply shining fetishes
for those ancestor deities
now soiled with my body
in consumptive ephemera

will they know me in this wreckage?

will the audience seek truth
will they murmur to one another as they surveil me
gorge on my suffering until it runs through their fingers?
will i hear them from all the way over here?

yes, they'll say, *clearly a very unhappy person*

their architecture

unwhole, gleaming, their edges are soft
sanded and ground to softness
near skinless
their flesh is open and wet
worn past translucence

hard and shining and whole
edges sharp with newness
they are columns, cathedrals
softnesses folded into geometries
untenable
light shines through

they cannot be held
or they will die

ape

for a brief time i was the very best animal
for the very best big boy
aping—a very special friend or silhouette
his divinity of brutalism
its own monstrous timothy treadwell-ism
white arctic runs—all crossing oaths
all savage heathens in any one row
of degenerate peers all nicknamed animal

petty crimes ever named grisly or polar
tracked and surveilled and tagged
videographers fetishizing a made-up wrongness
that they'll chase us miles for, to end up
displayed as heads in faraway lodges
us, adorning their houses

a future awaits them waking every day
to paint on caricatures of our stolen faces
never having known us ever

when i get too old for this assembly line of worth

i still won't get the meadow
they will catch on to my little charms

i'm no donation in body to experience
or theory—and have given no veal
inhabiting the shell of an unproductive body
my bones crack every which way i move
a half jacket half suffered in value—my greatest pride
in the end i'll come to nothingness and
lay in the cool earth with my effects

when they pull me down by my feet
cutting me into my parts and discarding what the earth saw
my juice and flesh, my knowing arm
with its every atrophied nerve
in permanent poor ends

i will generously bequeath myself to the state
let them feed on my tumorous gristle
leave the rest to this dead earth
leave the best to the smallest maggots

sun pharaoh

ignorant, five hours late for a date
my accepted excuse was a puppy
we didn't see that basquiat show for a minute
uh, a brooklyn sort, UN mom type
i don't know what that means, but you do
i used to dread seeing him scroll up on my dash

ubiquitous red swim trunks
smiling his subtle bullshit
always some faraway, warmer
different better maybe than here place
here being probably my bed
or the rest of my life a waiting room
my bed in that i live my life there now
pray, break bread, hold testimony

he didn't care
i sought his assessment of my lack
later i'd look for him online
needy for indifference, i'd eat just that
i liked seeing him far away anyway

some love you better by not, and apathetically
the reward of him not giving a damn had me unshackled
after a time trapped in the rib cages of others

him drinking perpetually before noon
dreaming without urgency
never motivated to hold me ever
free and brushing free off on me
                    sad, the same as anyone
                                        the same as us
                    a homemade sun, like those little plastic fans
                    letting it shine on me

under his sleepy gaze i could be anyone
i craved that and its namelessness
a year spent collecting the sun

and promises we knew he'd never keep
to bring bottles of shine back to me

self-taught

content warning: sexual violence

some men don't have to use force
to get their way, kings and murderers are alike
the promise of force is enough reverb
everyone blooms for promises
we unfurl for fear, drink it

my eyes kept drifting to the corner
he had a closet in the back of his room
with a dirty sheet hanging for a curtain
where we weren't allowed to go
man, what is a gun, anyway?

i will venture further into the dark

where were the alarm bells when his hand clamped down on me
in the pitch black?

was this what we came for?
and not for the roof to see the stars?
little too hard just under my jaw
awareness creeps up in a heat wave

but this is already away from me, a wave

i'm warm and not too smart
i can't remember what happens
between that heat and the dark

i will venture further

his friend my cousin came and found me there
tired, i fought like i was brand new
in the dark i don't think i made a sound
i was dancing—pushing at the pain with my feet
some people are too strong, caricatures of strength
some people are made to show you how weak you are

my sister was there too
who knows what she saw, did
had done, done to
she is not my story

we share a special power
we can use magic to bless events
and turn everything into a game
or a story, a staged play, a drama

in the dawn we'll go to my aunt's house
reeking of violent men

cigarettes that our friends smoke that we
swear we never tasted

alcohol that we never drank
we are too good for that

full up on black coils of shame
expiring in tanti's same house

we were ripe before, now we are spoiled

i didn't think he knew about his friend, my cousin
he invited me over to smoke days later
why i returned we'll still wonder
boredom? confusion? a wish to rewrite events
stupidity? idiocy? folly?

there's his chauffeur sitting in the driveway
in a plastic lawn chair, damn bored—nowhere to go

nowhere to go but up stairs—i gotta go up three flights
each story a story about the war

(see this big pretty house—falling apart and rotten
the seeds of this fruit are black flies
since the war nobody eats anything touched by black flies
we all know that they were crowding
in the crevices of the eyes of corpses
not long before they expired in your guinness)

the maids are there, them with nowhere to go
they barely get paid, mostly fed
a steel sliver above slave   can and can't leave any time
i can leave any time, but i don't

i swear this is where i learn for real (it's not)
i set the trap and i walk into it
i'm here to visit a friend

after, when he holds me down just under my jaw, throat too tight
i know then that they're all friends, it's all the same game
when they all come in one by one
they are like soldiers marching

d-a, and b, and s who calls
bb, his friend, my cousin
who lives just down the way
one by one and another

til i bleed from one knee to the other
it didn't happen if there aren't pictures
if you didn't get a t-shirt
don't remember

astonished, i will mistake their offer
to run my torn dress to the tailor
for a kindness

i taught me everything i needed to know
about myself
those maids hear me screaming?
did i make a sound?

months later when i don't have any sort of illness
i feel so lucky and i brag
that orgy that i had last spring makes me daring
i learned it all
so that's what i mean when i say that i am

self-educated

and some people hurt themselves with objects
but men are like objects
to me

denouement:

(two years later i go back to my auntie's house and his friend my cousin bb is at the convenience store and i'm so sick i can barely move and while i stand there frozen he kisses my cheek and says m took up with some white girl and she flew him to miami to get married, forever her mandingo)

heroics

how could i refuse

the unrequested slide of

the skin of strange men who use

my body to prop up their exchanges

they are forever

shaking hands

on my thighs

posturing

on my cheeks

kneeling

at my feet

i am furniture and i am a throne

my voice is that pretty music

accompanying heroics

blurry

the fire eating all this shrapnel is imaginary
we are not in a trapped car, they'll say
we will side eye these armoured bodies of the state
post-state, post-language, lullaby copywriters
these are sedatives, dulling agents
enshrined in old books encased in institutions
enshrouded in clouds on the top of mountains

you'll have to give in
for the innocence to sneak in, they'll say
you will cut out your own eyes
before you put the wool on
look at you, desire for oblivion

dirt obsessions give in, they'll say

give in to muted blurry mornings
while you traverse the plain
of your own fruitlessness
on all fours
feeling forward, a path

folded paper hands unreliable

they'll say

there's the dirt
there's the rub
here's the dirt

let the strangers pollute your aura
sell your data, consent to its nebulous use
write them permission slips, check boxes
yes, feed me, check, soothe me, check
arsenic stone fruit pitted at houses
will make them look bulleted

and, anyway
they'll say

you already know
you have to kill yourself
in order to survive this

sometimes

they call it a haunting
when i was a baby they called it old eyes

it's a tiredness
all this bloodletting

now there are only my forest pathways
my temple steps, tree veins
there used to be a

kind of
blankness

that would come over me sometimes that
made it so i had to work

a little harder than other people to be
warm or
care

keener

regressing into reflective apartment buildings
is a keen professional imaginer of maybes
an eager to lessen the blow's echo type

i am present but my presence is convalescing
the borders of me blur with little intervention
my yield to contamination is expedient
call it an aura leak or sponsored erasure
i've been romanced by invisibility from time now

i crave my unbeing syrup and taste less
    i want my labour to lose my value
        let only me spend me, puff me, pass
    sew myself up less   i be the steel beams

once they see your ribs you're an automaton
wounds are for deer and cattle
slow to heal leads you to the slaughter

a quick interruption of polyfill gets you to the next round
  i am soft to impact absorbing blows
  i want to break that fall
  betting on metal bones would empty me

  i am not the type
  i use brown liner like an illustrious shield
  carve an eight-hour smile into the corners of my mouth

        set out hunting for a temporary rest stop
        any house on this block is a rest stop in a rush

  find me, enamoured by the tile in all these homes
    homes nervous, oscillating trembling walls
  window eyes look across to sharp lined churches
      next slide opens with a sharp sweep of mink
      the swift diversion is in danger of causing
        convulsions in a perfectly
      ordinary division of the population
      just live in the right place
      move at the right pace
      be lucky

do you know that the game lasts the longest
longest in a little home with a bit of heat and lemon?
and crumbs and crits of dust i've named and blessed?
and nowhere to make amends to the shadows in corners
let's be friends

a soured mouth wrinkled up inner pink cavern
is evidence of a good meal and learned lesson
madness will let you romance anything if you let it
stockholm syndrome

watch me try to learn that lesson
our morals are blurry, the crossovers staggering
hyperbolic, we signal our virtues with death matches
blurriness carrying over to the truth industry
opaques a curtain of ink diluting every photo i'm in

and every photo i'm in is tagged with my ambivalence
i reach in and smudge me—i blacken me

it's that economic lie
it's that federal ideation tax

it's that soft thump in the night

caught on flash

i'm a new me i'm a new me

i'm a new me

i'm new

autodeity

i haven't yet climbed down the mountain
an aberration lives here in earnest
hanging in the air and after imprint of me
crystal light castles, fine silhouettes
any stone formed under pressure
can have a million faces

i am a million faces
i've lived so many births i'm dizzy
a great wide animal bit out a piece
of my vertebrae, replaced it with thorns

i wasn't born in a womb
i slid out the pussy of a papaya
i am the fresh new leaf
of a dozen thousands of fruits and flowers

there used to be two of me, identical twins
but different sexes, i ate them
we ate each other—ourobouros brothers

i am a dormant weapon
i'm still dreaming up new wars

look for me and my many million lovers
i won't remember a one just them as one

i won't remember care i'll remember caring
i'll forget being held, only not withholding

i'll never be smarter than this
                                        a blessing

all i know is grow, drink root, mash rot
i'm an uprooted plant
                                                dry air
                i've not had enough water or sunlight
                                                        to grow true
                        they'll hang me upside down to death
                                                        to preserve me

        i am powdered into dreams for others
                i am a medicine, i am power

every six months i shed my skin

and become new and pure, another
i spontaneously forget any language but my own
finally everyone admits i'm incomprehensible

thirty years from now i'll die
by submerging myself in very cold water
this will be the first of many deaths
of my many voluntary surrenders

my gown will be weighed with jewels
and will float me to the bottom where
i'll wait a thousand years to surface
having forgotten all of this i'll be new
newer than ever, better

a monolithic ultraviolet stone will be dropped in the desert
i'll find it and submerge myself in the stone like a mineral bath

people will travel for days and bow to me for days
and come away unable to touch the ground with their feet

(they'll float forever)

i don't need a come down
i just get higher and higher

i never climb down
i become the mountain

In Acknowledgement

This book is a surprise. It is a collection of poems that didn't know they were poems. I would write these in the notes of my phone on my way to and from jobs.

AJR, my loyal friend, asked to see these poems, and published some of them, so that I could bring you the rest here today.

RHG liked those and got this manuscript to Brick Books. They spoke up for me, and encouraged me to be demanding, and I was.

AM abandoned emailing and graciously texted me so that I could summon up the executive function to finish this book. The trust she has shown me has been instrumental to this work.

TONGO didn't know who I was and accepted my request to be mentored by him. He gave me rituals, routes, powers. I will never be the same poet again. I have been deeply humbled.

TB made a little world with me, letting me cry all the time. My beloved friend. I truly cannot stand you.

YA, I wrote this book in great part for the community of knowing we share. You are one of my truest siblings. I love you to the end of the earth.

To my mother, I owe perhaps the most thanks, who made like some wild animals do, leaving their young in the forest to make them strong. I am free of wondering if you love me.

Assiyah Jamilla Touré is a multidisciplinary artist of West African descent. They were born and raised on Skwxwú7mesh land and lived for many years in Kanien'kehà:ka territory (Montreal) and are now based on the lands of the Mississaugas of the Anishinaabe, the Haudenosaunee Confederacy and the Wendat (Toronto). In 2018 their chapbook *feral* was published by House House Press. *Autowar* is their first full-length collection.